Foundations of Freemasonry Series

Four Lesser-Known Masonic Essays

Foundations of Freemasonry Series

Four Lesser-Known Masonic Essays

by Frank C. Higgins

Lamp of Trismegistus
NEW YORK . GENEVA . BEIJING
WELLINGTON . KANSAS CITY

Copyright © 2013 Lamp of Trismegistus

All rights reserved. No part of this publication may be reproduced or transmitted in any form or by any means, electronic or mechanical, including photocopying, recording, or by any information storage and retrieval system, without permission in writing from Lamp of Trismegistus. Reviewers may quote brief passages.

ISBN: 978-1-63118-003-3

Contents

A Definition of Masonry
The American Freemason, December 1912

Masonic Archeology
The Builder, January 1915

The Meaning of Initiation
The Builder, July 1916

The Two Ashlars
The Builder, December 1916

Introduction

A favorite among his scholarly peers at the time, fellow masonic author, Joseph Fort Newton (*and editor of the Builder*) had this to say about Bro. Higgins:

More than once we have called attention, editorially and otherwise, to the admirable work of Brother Frank C. Higgins, of the Magician Society, New York, in his department of Masonic Research in the Masonic Standard. At first it began as a column of inquiry and answer dealing with the Deeper Problems of the meaning of Masonry, but it grew, most happily, into a series of systematic studies, or lessons-- Masonry, as Brother Higgins conceives it, being the perpetuation among us, albeit little understood, of the ancient philosophy of Cosmic Harmony which, among the Hebrews, traced everything to the great Jehovah; at once a religious and a scientific pursuit, conducted along mathematical, geometrical and astronomical lines. In this field Brother Higgins is a master, and comes nearer than anyone with whose work we are acquainted, making the treasures of that rich but difficult culture intelligible to the average reader. In order to call attention again to his researches, and also to express the hope that they may be gathered into permanent form, we venture to reproduce two brief sections of his series of studies dealing with the meaning of initiation. This Society keeps an open and responsive heart toward all its fellow-workers, glad and grateful for any one who toils to make our great and many-sided Masonry more intelligible and effective.

A DEFINITION OF MASONRY

In his facetious search for a "Brand New Theory of Masonic Origins" in last February's *American Freemason*, the Editor "found all countries and nations of antiquity preempted. Paradise, the Garden of Eden, Egypt, India, Ancient Britain and prehistoric America had been exploited, while Gymnosophists, Buddhists, Tibetan Lamas, Chinamen, Mayas, Incas, Benedictine Monks and Jesuit Fathers had been laid under contribution, and each heralded in turn as responsible for the beginnings of Masonry.

The writer is but too familiar with the resources of Masonic bibliography not to feel sympathetically akin to the shepherd lad "with his sling and five small stones from a brook," who sallied forth to meet the giant Philistine; but like David of old he does not despair of returning with the head of the giant problem which will never cease to puzzle humanity until it is adequately worked out.

The purpose of this paper is less to enter point blank upon the labyrinthine paths of solution than to define the exact character of the "riddle of the ages" and hazard a theory of how it may or can, - yes, has been solved.

The growing body of students of comparative religion, who term themselves "Theosophists," have a precisely similar difficulty to cope with, and as among interested Masonic students, hundreds are at work endeavoring to localize and historicize principles which are ever elusive, because the truth concerning them is that they are everywhere manifest and have been so during all time. The beginning of Masonry cannot he found, for the precise reason that "before Abraham was, Masonry is."

That which Masonry searches, that which Theosophy searches, that which dogmatic religion fears to search, or rather fears the discovery of, is one and the self-same thing. Theosophy, for want of a better term, calls it the "Ancient Wisdom," and is in a measure right, but not even Theosophy has fully grasped the specific identity of the lost science of the Logos.

And yet, Theosophy is full of it, Masonry is full of it and the religions of the world are full of it; full of its fragments, its unidentified debris, its mutilated fractions, scattered like those of Osiris upon the waves.

"Paradise" and Noah's Ark are indeed part of it and the Creation epic of Hawaii is but an echo of that of Babylon.

There is a LAW, so simple in itself and in its applications that the veriest child may be made to comprehend its lessons, by which the Universe unfolds like a plant from within the germ heart of its seed, and to man exhibits, as though upon an unrolled scroll, all those marvelous philosophies which have conferred immortality upon the Sages of Hellas and the Orient.

This LAW reveals at once the nature of our Creator; enough of the bent of His infinite mind for us to be assured that our own finite natures are truly reflexes of the

Divine prototype, so that the assurance that "God made man in His own image" ceases to be but pointless babble.

It reveals, by the minute and incontrovertible testimonies which it gives to that effect, that all of the historical mythologies and religious philosophies which the world has ever harbored were originally designed as exoteric, recordable veils for esoteric, unrevealable, unrecordable FACTS, classed today as "Mysteries," not as unknowable but as unknown.

The "keeping of this LAW," in the aspirational, emotional, sacrificial sense, even though it be today unidentified except as a vague longing of the human heart for a reality which is sensed rather than comprehended, is RELIGION.

The knowledge of this LAW, the power to grasp and apply it, to consciously and knowingly work, hand in hand, with the G.A.O.T.U., to live in a close bond of union with an ever present Master, and realize that physical death is but loving initiation to a loftier degree, was once

MASONRY.

Religion was the promise, Masonry the pledge.

That pledge exists to-day enshrined in every Lodge, for he who can penetrate behind the veil may read in every sign and symbol the story and the reason of his being. As beautiful and inspiring as is the Masonic ritual and as full of manifest heart-searching truth as it may be, it has been completely voided of its ancient science. Many of its monitorial injunctions, though full of benevolence and solicitude for the brother, are vapid and unhistoric or unscientific. It has become a species of religion also, to be taken on faith in statements which make no tax upon the understanding.

Yet Masonry and Religion are children of the same divine parentage. Alike, each had its rise in a precise, God-communicated fund of practicable, ponderable fact. This is the reason for the universality of symbolisms.

The salient features of the ancient

Mysteries of various lands in which initiations were the requisites of practical worship, as differentiated from mere prayers, offerings and sacrifices in full light of day, have been ably handled by several generations of Masonic writers, but the nature of the superior information conveyed to the high initiate has not only eluded discovery, and in most cases no suspicion has been entertained by modern writers that there was any more to the ceremonies of the ancient Mysteries than a sort of super-heated Italian apprentisaggio, which taught the neophyte wholesome respect for the power of his order.

It is upon this point that we base our dissent from the theory that the controversy anent Masonic origins be closed, because we are personally convinced that it has not even yet begun.

In expectation of further light on this interesting topic, we may be permitted to hazard a few hints as to the direction from which it may be anticipated.

There is not a symbol or article of

furniture in the Lodge which has not a reason for its shape, size, number, (if plural) and presence, utterly outside of and transcending the monitorial explanation thereof, as a scientific demonstration of which the moral deduction gives no hint whatsoever.

The higher the degree, the more this divergence becomes apparent, for while the symbolism becomes more expressive and claims to embody more subtle teachings, it fails to convey to initiates therein certain positive knowledge, the possession of which would raise them head and shoulders above the lewd of non-initiates, intellectually, without reference to the resonance of their titles or the size of their medals or jewels.

This knowledge, which was the fruit of ancient initiations was not only positive, but practical.

It would enable a single individual to give arts, letters and science to a race of nomad barbarians within the space of his own life-time, and the semi-myths of

Hermes, Thoth, Cadmus, Oannes, Fo-Hi and others who are enshrined in the histories of ancient peoples as having actually done so, are but embodiments of the truth that it was of a superior manner of imparting practical knowledge and the impressing of such as the direct gift of God, made manifest as the giver entitled to the gratitude and claiming it, that initiation consisted.

The universality of these "first civilizer" myths therefore direct our attention to the possibility of a teaching capable of transforming the poor, blind and ignorant, wherever found, into masters of the work of civilization and enlightenment by process of initiation, rather than education, although the one is the corollary of the other.

To the universality of the "Teacher" myths must be added the universality of the majority of Masonic symbols, which as we have noted, are being pointed out under every sky as proof positive that whatever it was, which has since become

Masonry, originated at that latitude and longitude.

We have therefore to halt in our wild globe scurry after the site of the legendary Masonic "Garden of Eden" and realize that in pursuit of something of which we find the prehistoric traces EVERYWHERE, coupled with traditions of Divine origin, we may have to recast our notions and refocus our binoculars upon some principle or set of correlated principles which express the same things to all peoples, times and places, because they are eternal verities and not mere toys. Now the astonishing part of it all is that Masonry possesses this marvelous treasure and do" not know it.

"He came unto his own and they knew him not," applies with as great force to the pseudo Jew of the Lodge as to the racial Jew of be "promised land."

The Masonic ritual of the civilized world bespeaks a line of descent more particularly from the Jewish deposit of the "Ancient Wisdom," than from, for example, the Chinese or the Aztec.

Therefore we will probably not go far astray in tracing our ritualistic development along that historical line of racial progress.

The history of the Jewish people is something widely apart from the trash taught with the avowed object of fastening the crime of the ages upon the heads of this people.

Their historical contacts with Persia, Babylonia and Egypt during both Pharaohonic and Ptolemaic times and their contacts with Greek philosophy must be placed in the balance.

We must not forget that the Old Testament of the Christian was translated not from the "Torah," but from the copied "Pentateuch," a work which filled the orthodox Jewish world, at the time the original translation was made, with horror, because the Egyptian-Greek-Hebrew rabbis who made it injected therein the glyphs of the secret philosophy of the Sun-priests of Heliopolis, so that Kohaleth, son of David, surnamed "Shelomoh," "the Prince of Peace," became for all time Sol-Om-On, "The Sun, breathing life upon Heliopolis," and the fundamental principles of the Babylonian Kabbalah, or number philosophy of the ancient Magi, which the Torah already embodied, applied to the construction of proper names, extended so as to make them conceal a sort of Baconian cipher of the "Wisdom of the Egyptians," a system which develops in excelsis in the subsequent construction of the "New Testament."

That this cipher is a concealment of the true meanings of the symbols of the Masonic Lodge and the revelation of the LAW to which they bear witness, of its Divinity, of its globe-encircling universality, and of its eternal truth, it is the promise of the immediate future to make manifest.

MASONIC ARCHAEOLOGY

With reference to all those things which come within the various provinces of the seven liberal arts and sciences, Masonry occupies an extremely anomalous position. The theory of the Craft we all know. From one degree to another, we have paraded before us, assumptions of all knowledge, human and Divine. We are supposed to be the custodians of a mysterious arcana descended to us from remote ages, which must be hedged about with safeguards and pledges, which could not be more exacting, if they constituted a system of defense for the fabled treasures of Golconda, actually materialized.

Yet there is not a Masonic student, among those hold enough to proclaim that there is at least a substratum of truth at the bottom of these pretensions, who does not find himself continually in the minority, among a vast army of brethren, who refuse to contemplate anything in the ritual of Masonry, transcending an agreeable series of moral platitudes, collated within a comparatively modern period for the unmixed purpose of "making Masons."

The degrees of the Craft are, in this respect, very much like those honorary titles conferred by Universities upon benefactors, who, had they actually elected to shine in the domains of Law, Arts, Letters or Sciences, suggested by their alphabetical dignities, instead of Coal, Iron or Commerce would never have figured in the history of pedagogics as patrons of learning.

In consideration of the hugely preponderating part played by at least the presumption of Science in its construction, one might imagine that Masonry would have long since specially attracted to itself an unusual quota of scientific men, men of the schools, competent through predilection and training to give extension to the manifold hints of our ritual. But with notable exceptions, this has not proven the case.

The chief among Masonic students,

whose reputations for more or less scientific research into the latent meanings of Masonic allusions, have become classic in the Craft, have been gifted amateurs, who have no reputation outside of our exclusive ranks. Such science as has been brought to the support of Masonry has been purely accidental. Owing to the nature of our institution, we are unable to turn for guidance to the very men who could most and best enlighten us. We may take no, however learned, scientist into Masonic confidence and invite him to diagnose a landmark, having a pointed scientific application, for the benefit of the craft, unless he is a member thereof and the conflict between Science and Religion has, since the organization of the modern speculative craft, given rise to a special reason which has closed its doors to many of the very men who could have been most depended on to enlighten it.

For these and other reasons Masonic symbolism has remained for several centuries in the hands of brethren who, however lovable and amiable their personal characters, or however they have adorned the Craft by their personal virtues, have been the last men in the world to perceive either its origin or its tendencies on the purely intellectual plane. The progress of true Masonic enlightenment has therefore been slower than that of any branch of human contemplation open to examination, dissection and suggestion from unbiased scholars.

Brilliant as have been the many scholarly Protestant Divines who have given luster to Masonry by their high qualities as men and Masons, the majority of these have been content to regard the numerous scriptural allusions and parallels introduced to attention, from the literal and unquestioning attitude of sectarian orthodoxy. Thus it has remained for a future age to reveal many things, which might have been discovered and brought to light years ago, if there had been systematic search. The true story of humanity's struggle toward the light during the past twenty centuries of the Christian era has yet to be written. It involves elements which numerous historians have approached closely enough, but which they have never been able to grasp, because of fundamental error in view point.

For nigh upon two thousand years, the true nature and meanings of the ancient mysteries upon which modern Masonry has erected her symbolic Temple, have remained in the grasp and custody of an institution, equally founded upon them, which has employed every artifice of sophistry to conceal and every instrument of physical repression to guard from the assaults of the curious. The history of this conflict is the history of "Heresy," concerning which we will sum the whole in one all embracing statement.

The entire totality of the various historical heresies which are recorded as having been subdued at one and another age of the Church, have been simply outcroppings of one and the same original gnosis, under different names, until the translations of the Bible into vulgar tongues, produced a new variety of schism, shifting the controversial premises from the original ground, which dealt with the Mysteries alone, to questions of historicity and literal interpretations of an unassailable Scripture, all sense of the cabalistic character of which had been hopelessly lost.

The battle of the last two centuries has raged altogether around questions affecting the total or partial authenticity of the Biblical narrative taken as a record of human history rendered infallible by Divine interference. Its uncompromising literal interpretations, the strict Puritan sense, have given rise to a long line of splendidly intellectual, but less misguided than unguided materialists, whose violent attitudes, in opposition to so called "revealed" religion, were provoked by the stubborn and uncompromising defense of sticklers for the historical veracity of a thousand physically impossible and completely unnatural narratives. That these narratives might have a concealed sense and convey the spiritual lessons of the "ancient mysteries" of their derivation, no more flashed across the minds of men like Voltaire, Thomas Paine, or to come down to our own day, Robert G. Ingersoll, than over those of Martin Luther or John Calvin.

To recapitulate the influences which have resulted in the gradual readjustment of the situation, rescuing us from the danger of a sullen and uncompromising conflict between the grossest and most blasphemous negation of Divinity and a blind Credence, in the exercise of which man must stand ready to surrender every prompting of reason or God-given common sense, would be to largely recapitulate the work which has been slowly and painfully accomplished within the ranks of the Masonic craft since the emergency of speculative Masonry from its underground crypt, under the liberal institutions of Protestant England, Germany, and later, of Republican France.

Scholarly Masons, who are duly

qualified, did fail to recognize likenesses between Masonic terminologies and traditions of the Ancient Mysteries preserved in the Greek classics and in the allusions of early alchemistic and "magical" writings. This led to an examination of innumerable hints contained in the homilies of the early fathers, concerning the mysteries, both Pagan and Christian, of the early days of the Church. Like putting together, bit by bit, the pieces of an enormous "cut out" puzzle, fragment after fragment has been brought together and joined to the main body

    The labors of the Abbe Constant, known best by his pen name of Eliphas Levi, did more than anything else to acquaint the western mind with the precise nature of spiritual mysteries and ancient methods of concealment, in his exposition of the long, jealously guarded Jewish Kabbalah. Upon this imperfect beginning have been based the Masonic writings of the venerable Albert Pike and from the same inspiration and greatly amplified by independent research, the published works of Helena Petrovna Blavatsky, with whose theosophical conclusions we shall not, however, concern ourselves. They have, however, had great influence over subsequent Masonic writers-like Dr. Buck and the Rev. Charles H. Vail.

The labor of Oriental Students has thrown open to the world the treasure houses of ancient Zend, Sanskrit and Arabic literature, which have supplied the connecting links in the great story of the inception of an age old scientific gnosis, materially set forth to the western world in the philosophies of the ancient students of Eastern lore, Aristotle, Plato and Pythagoras. The work of the Assyriologists and Egyptologists has furnished other links to the chain, extending our vision and broadening its range, until we are brought face to face with a wonderful, new and magnificently supported conclusion--that the significant symbolism of this great institution of ours, was indeed selected at some remote period of human history and handed down for the express purpose of discovering to us the origin of man's highest spiritual contemplations, and to enable us like the fathers of our race to climb otherwise inaccessible heights and view our Creator "face to face."

The consensus of all that has been discovered in this respect develops the fact that, way back in the dawn of history, probably long before it, there originated at some point on earth's surface, (indications which point to Northern India are not lacking) a curiously interlocking geometrical, mathematical and astronomical gnosis.

From purely natural experiments was derived a conception of the three hundred and sixty degrees of the circle, triangle and quadrangular equations, by means of squares (the Mosaic pavement) and the equilateral triangle, the Alphabet and the Decimal system. Adding the factors of the perceptible phenomena of the Universe, the mutual relations of divers geometrical figures of equal quantities and the elements of organic generation, mainly as phallicism, a great system, intended to account for the wonders of Nature, was devised, credited to the One; Absolute Mind ruling the Universe and placed under the government of the College of primitive scientists, to which later ages gave the name of the Magi.

The only difference between elementary Masonry and Theosophy, is the assumption by the latter that the most spiritual of those men achieved successive reincarnations on increasing scales of Divine inspiration and possession, which led them, in the course of time, to become the founders of the world's greatest religions, and has perpetuated their conscious personalities, even to our own day, under the generic title of "the Masters." Both are children of the legendary "Secret Doctrine."

As a point of departure for the assumption of a special science of Masonic Archaeology, we are, while prepared to allow the most complete liberty of thought with regard to historic cities and anthropomorphic conceptions, compelled to assume that wherever the knowledge and attributes of God have been demonstrated by means of the Square and Compasses, for the purpose of awakening the spiritual sense latent in all mankind, there existed Masonry. With this single proposition in view, there is not an acre of earth's surface, at one time or another trodden by the foot of intelligent man, which does not furnish its countless mute testimonies to the existence and cultivation of the primordial gnosis, of which we speak, passed from race to race and land to land.

It does not consist in structural architectural remains alone, but in geometrical symbolisms and decorative ornaments, in which the proportions of edifices, the shape and dimensions of stones, the decorative features of Temples and supposed Idols, especially the Pyramidal forms of Egypt and America, are made, by the translations of their geometrical angles and proportions into mathematical quantities, to give the precise length of the Solar year, the period of the precession of the Equinoxes, the period of human gestation, important planetary cycles and other great natural facts. The expression of these same quantities and formulae in the letters of the ancient alphabets, represented by their numbers, compose the various sacred names of diverse scriptures of humanity, so that we rest stupefied before the astounding fact, that the greatest message of our own Great light has yet to be read through Masonic eyes, by the light of the Ages past.

Masonic Archaeology is no chimera, nor product of an exalted imagination. It can be read, character by character, on countless objects in the Museums of every country in the world, possessing such, on the facades of and in the proportions of ancient Temples, from Delphi to Delhi, from Athens to Angkor. The ancient monuments of Mexico are supercharged with it and the evidences that this gnosis was the faith and practice of the ancient, aboriginal inhabitants of these United States are incontrovertible.

It stares the craft in the face from every corner of lodge and Chapter, and every word, letter, syllable and character thereof is stamped with God's own signature, the ineffable Tetragrammaton.

The London times, in its issue of October 30th, has a most interesting sketch and appreciation of General Joffre, the Commander-in-Chief of the French armies - a simple man, quiet, efficient, who does his duty and does not talk about it. Incidentally, the writer tells us that General Joffre is an enthusiastic Freemason - a fact which will give an added interest to his achievements as a soldier of the republic.

THE MEANING OF INITIATION

In all ancient rites and mysteries the participants in which were received by initiation, the greatest care was always exercised with respect to certain details, which if not properly carried out might mar or invalidate the entire ceremony.

The true significance of all initiation has ever been that of a spiritual rebirth. The sacred Agrouchada of the Hindus says, "The first birth is merely the advent into material life; the second birth is the entrance to a spiritual life."

The newly initiated into the first degree of Brahmanism was called douidja, which means "twice born." The very word initiate indicates that the candidate is at least symbolically in the same situation as if he had had no previous existence. He is to be ushered into an altogether new world.

In ancient initiations the extremity of humility was expressed by the rent garments of contrition for past offenses in the life about to be blotted out, the bosom offered to the executioner's sword, and the attitude of a captive.

PREPARING THE CANDIDATE

The most curious custom perhaps had to do with what might be termed the complete preparation of the candidate against the influences that had affected his previous career. During the multitude of centuries in the course of which astrology was thought to play the strongest part in human affairs, every circumstance affecting the welfare of humanity was deemed to have its rise in one or another of the planets, or perhaps in a lucky or evil combination of several. The science of medicine rose entirely from this curious belief in planetary affinities. The ancient physician diagnosed his patient's malady according to the diseases listed under the latter's unlucky stars and tried to cure it by application of substances designated as governed by those planets favorable to him. The same idea governed the individual with reference to articles carried upon his person. The superstitious carried various charms and amulets intended to draw favorable planetary influences to his aid, and was just as careful to avoid substance that might produce a contrary effect.

In the ordering of the candidate for initiation into the ancient mysteries this belief played an important part. The candidate might carry upon his person nothing that would invite the attention of occult planetary powers through the mysterious tie that bound them to terrestrial objects.

METALLIC TOKENS

The lists of plants, flowers, minerals, metals, and other things that were subject to these mysterious influences were long and complicated. Gold linked him with the sun which incited to the besetting sin of intellectual pride; silver drew upon him the fickle qualities of the moon; copper, sacred to Venus, provoked lust, and iron, the metal of Mars, quarrelsomeness; tin, tyranny and oppression, the qualities of Jupiter; lead, sloth and indolence, belonging to Saturn; while mercury or quicksilver was responsible for dishonesty and covetousness. Therefore a key or a coin, and above all a sword, was likely to bring confusion upon the whole mysterious operation of regeneration.

Above all were enjoined upon the candidate the three sacred virtues, which by the Jain sects in India are still called "the three jewels," represented by three circles, "right belief," "right knowledge," and "right conduct." In order to reach the spiritual plane, in which the soul is entirely freed from the bonds of matter, these were the chief necessities, and the person who clung to them would certainly go higher until he reached the state of liberation.

THREE REGULAR STEPS

To the ancient candidate were also recommended "the three successive steps which open the soul to free and unobstructed activity and communication on both the psychic and the spiritual planes." The first was to still the ego and empty the mind of every bias and standard of self and sense. The second consisted, when this passive state had been induced, in fixing and holding the attention upon the specific object about which the truth was desired.

Thirdly, the foregoing two steps having been taken, the individual was to stand firmly and persistently in the receptive and listening attitude for the immediate revelation of the truth, in the full expectation of getting it. This receptive state and expectant attitude opened the consciousness to "the psychic vibrations that write unerringly their story on the receptive mind."

WHOM DOES THE CANDIDATE REPRESENT?

Within the simple and easily formulated problem asked in the heading is contained the sublimest of all secrets, which various of the higher degrees have sought to answer, each in its own way. It involves the intimate application of all the symbolic degrees to the initiate himself, without which they are as empty as air.

In all the ancient mysteries a character was assumed by the candidate, and as the candidates were any and the character depicted always the same, it must have represented something essentially common to all alike. Furthermore, the precise similarity of the experiences to which each individual candidate was subjected argued the identical lesson in all cases.

Examination of all available detail, especially the sacred writings of many races, confirms us in the conviction that this universal character was but an allegorical representation of the ego or "self," engaged in the warfare of which it has been said that the victor is greater than he who taketh a city" and emerging a conqueror in the very instant of apparent defeat. We receive our earliest concrete presentation of such a character in the celebrated document known as the Egyptian Book of the Dead, the Bible of the builders of the Pyramids, fragments of which are found wrapped in the cloths of almost every mummy.

THE PILGRIM SOUL

The Book of the Dead presents the wanderings of a departed soul through the underworld to the council of the gods, who were to listen to its accusers, give heed to its defenders, and finally weigh its accumulated good deeds in the scales against the feather symbol of "truth." The name of this character is given as Ani the Scribe. It finally transpired that this name was equivalent to the Latin term ego, meaning the "I Am" or "self" in man. This leads to what was perhaps the greatest and most important of all secret teachings of the ancient world, one that has become so obscured by the confusion of its many dramatic representations with real historical characters,--that most clear and careful labor is required to trace the main ideas from age to age and people to people, in order to show that they are fundamentally everywhere exactly the same.

There is no difficulty whatever in recognizing the self-conscious principle in every man as being an actual spark of the infinite self-consciousness precipitated into material existence, through the labyrinth of which it is compelled to strive in ceaseless search for the Master's Word, the secret of its being and immortal destiny. If this idea of the struggle of a divine and immortal soul, weighed down with the burden of matter and assailed at every turn by foes that symbolize the continual transformations of matter from "life" to "death" and "death" to "life," be taken as the vital principle of every drama of regeneration, from the "Book of the Dead" to John Bunyan's "Pilgrim Progress," we too shall have progressed a long way upon the road to understanding that of Freemasonry.

THE PILOT STAR

The beautiful star that is the chief emblem of the Royal Arch degree, besides being the sacred symbol of Israel, has had no other meaning during the thousands of years from the most ancient Brahmanism to the Temple of today. Even when called "the United Seal of Vishnu and Siva," the "Immortal" and the "Mortal," or "Fire" the symbol of Spirit, and "Water" the symbol of Matter, it represented the same idea, that of the "Self Conqueror," the Perfect Man, who had learned the subjugation of human passions and perfection in attitude toward God and fellow man. Thus the up pointing triangle stood for the ascent of matter into spirit which is typified by the phrase "resurrection of the body," and the down-pointing triangle the descent of spirit into matter, and the complete star represents the immortal being fitted to dwell in "that house not built with hands, eternal in the heavens."

THE TWO ASHLARS

Our lodge is in every respect a symbolic workshop, furnished with all the tools belonging to the different grades of workmen, and with a trestle board upon which are set forth the day's designs and the material upon which the labor of the brethren is to be expended.

This symbolic material consists of the two ashlars, emblematic of the crude material and the finished product, which are placed plainly enough on view in New York lodges, but absent or almost unknown except to students in many other states. The oblong stones and nondescript slabs sometimes seen are noteworthy evidence that the age-old significance of the "cubical stone," which has played such a prominent role in the mythology and mysticism of the past, has almost run to oblivion in the modern craft. These stones should really be perfect cubes. The symbolism of the working tools is completely lost the moment such proportions are lost sight of or ignored. The ancient

Hebrews had their own version of the great "number philosophy," which lent sanctity and expressiveness to the number 12. First of all, it was the number of their Twelve Tribes, who were doubtless a symbolical enrolment of all the heads of families under the zodiacal sign of the month in which they were born. It is certainly significant that the patriarchal system was founded upon this number, and later on many other dispositions were made that showed a particular reverence for the Chaldean plan of the universe based upon 12 signs. As one cube possesses six sides each of which is a perfect square, a number of remarkable mathematical and geometrical symbolisms were established based upon the fact that all the numbers, from one to 12 added together produce 78. This number is also the sum of 3 times "26," the numerical value of the "Great and Sacred Name of Jehovah" (JHVH).

As each cube possesses 12 edges, the combined number require a 24-inch rule to symbolize their total outline. The breaking into different mathematical combinations of this supreme number, each significant of some one of the great ruling phenomena of nature, was seen in the symbolism of the use of an operative Mason's gavel in the dressing of building stones.

The grand old mystery name of our Creator, called the Tetragrammaton (Greek for "four-letter name") had as its root the three letters J, H, and V, which as numbers were 10, 5, and 6, or 21, the sum of the added numbers 1 to 6 represented by a single cube.

This fact was made the basis of a curious legend, ought by the wise old rabbis into that marvelous compilation called the Talmud, from which more than a little of our Masonic material has been derived.

The story is of the Patriarch Enoch (Hanok, father Methuselah), whose name means "the initiator," 10, all accounts agree, lived 365 years, or a "year of years." A remarkable book attributed to him is often alluded to by the Hebrew commentators and early Christian "Fathers"; but no trace of it was ever found until in the last century it turned up in Abyssinia. It has been translated out of that strange African dialect into many tongues. The so-called Book of Enoch contains a remarkable recital of astronomical science as known to the ancients, told entirely in allegorical form, while the history of the Children of Israel is prophesied under the allegorical simile of the remarkable doings of a singularly intelligent flock of sheep which build a house for their shepherd, the whole reading very much like a children's fairy tale.

The Talmudic legend of Enoch represents him as greatly disturbed at the news of the impending world Deluge," for fear the Name of God should be lost. He accordingly caused it to be inscribed upon a triangular plate of gold, and affixed it to a cubical stone, for the safe keeping of which he caused a series of nine arched vaults to be constructed, one beneath another, at the foot of Mt. Moriah (the holy mountain of the Jews, as Mt. Meru was of the Hindus). The rains came and the flood descended, and so washed the mud and silt over the site that it became completely obliterated.

Centuries later, when King David was moved "to build an house unto the Lord," and actually set his workmen to dig the foundations thereof, the latter discovered the vaults, and descending therein brought to light the long-buried stone.

Tradition also has it that the material of this stone was agate, which would at once connect it with the Hermetic philosophy; for agate, above all, was sacred to Hermes and Thoth or David. The latter, having been a warlike monarch, was not permitted to achieve that which he had begun and so bequeathed the cubical stone to his son Solomon, who made use of it as the cornerstone of the Temple.

The imagery of this is plain enough in the fact that, not in a written or engraved inscription, but in the mathematical proportions of the cube itself, was to be found that wonderful Name which is, as it were, the foundation of the universe, of which man is a fleshly epitome and the Temple on Mt. Moriah a symbolic one.

By knowing the use of the working tools of an E. A. the initiate might begin his labor of hewing and shaping the brute matter at his feet into stones fit for the builders' use; but when he had accomplished his task he was apprised that the symmetry and order it represented in its finished shape was "God": not a god whom he created, but a God whom his patient labor had revealed.

The cube itself was an age-old symbol of the spiritual Man, as set forth in the Mahabharata of ancient India:

> *A portion of Mine own Self, transformed in the world of life into an immortal Spirit, draweth round itself the senses of which the Mind, is the Sixth, veiled in Matter.*

Therefore we find the cube present in all the ancient mythologies, which were but racial cloaks for one and the same wisdom religion, understood by the priests of all countries alike as a symbol of the sixth sign of the zodiac, the characters portraying the great Mother of Wisdom and her divine son Man.

It is the task of the apprentice to break through the shell of matter and liberate the Divine Word that dwells within by opening his own spiritual perceptions to the light of the Logos. As the priceless statues of Phidias and Praxiteles were once shapeless masses of unmeaning stone and the Parthenon a sea-worn crag, until gavel and gage, mallet and chisel, in the hand of inspiration had performed their tasks, so has always been the lesson of the cube in its unshapen and shapen forms to the apprentice Mason.

www.ingramcontent.com/pod-product-compliance
Lightning Source LLC
LaVergne TN
LVHW091320080426
835510LV00007B/575